·EXQUISITE·
Calligraphuck
·EXPLETIVES·

ISBN 978-1-4521-2584-8
Manufactured in China.
Design by Linus Boman.

See the full range of Calligraphuck stationery products
at www.chroniclebooks.com.
For more from Calligraphuck, visit
www.calligraphuck.com

Chronicle Books publishes distinctive books and gifts.
From award-winning children's titles, bestselling
cookbooks, and eclectic pop culture to acclaimed works
of art and design, stationery, and journals, we craft
publishing that's instantly recognizable for its spirit
and creativity. Enjoy our publishing and become part
of our community at www.chroniclebooks.com.

20 19 18 17 16 15

CHRONICLE BOOKS

680 Second Street
San Francisco, CA 94107
www.chroniclebooks.com

WWW.CHRONICLEBOOKS.COM

$9.95 U.S. / £8.99 U.K.

ISBN 978-1-4521-2584-8

50995